Two folk tales

Illustrated by Steve Smallman

The lion and the mouse
page 2

Mr Rabbit and the moon
page 10

Nelson

The lion and the mouse

The big lion was sleeping.
A little mouse got on
the lion.

The little mouse
ran up and down.
"I can play on the lion,"
she said.

The lion got up.
"I will eat you, little mouse,"
he said.

"No, no," said the mouse.

"Let me go.

I can help you."

The big lion let the mouse go.

One day the lion
was trapped in a net.
"Help, help," he said.
"Can you help me?"

"I can't help you,"
said the monkey.
"I can't help you,"
said the snake.

"I can help you,"
said the little mouse.

The little mouse bit
the net and
the big lion got out.

"Thank you, little mouse,"
he said.
"You did help me."

Mr Rabbit and the moon

Mr Rabbit went down the road.
He saw a pool of water.
"I will look in the water,"
said Mr Rabbit.
"I will see if I look good."

Mr Rabbit looked in the water.
He did look good but
the moon was in the water.

"The moon is in the water," said Mr Rabbit.

"Come and look, Mrs Mole."

Mrs Mole looked in the water.
"The moon is in the water,"
said Mrs Mole.
"Come and look, Mr Rat."

Mr Rat looked in the water.
"The moon is in the water,"
said Mr Rat.
"Come and look, Mrs Owl."

Mrs Owl looked in the water.

"Look up," said Mrs Owl.

"The moon is not in the water."

Mr Rabbit, Mrs Mole and Mr Rat looked up.
The moon was in the sky.
"We are silly," they said.